WITHDRAWN
W9-BGR-877

Mysterious Encounters

Crop Circles

by Jan Burns

KIDHAVEN PRESS
A part of Gale, Cengage Learning

Detroit • New York • San Francisco • New Haven, Conn • Waterville, Maine • London

LIBRARY OF CONGRESS CATALOGING-IN-PUBLICATION DATA

Burns, Jan.
Crop circles / by Jan Burns.
p. cm. — (Mysterious encounters)
Includes bibliographical references and index.
ISBN 978-0-7377-4047-9 (hardcover)
1. Crop circles—Juvenile literature. 2. Curiosities and wonders—Juvenile literature. I. Title.
AG243.B788 2008
001.94—dc22

2008003810

KidHaven Press
27500 Drake Rd
Farmington Hills MI 48331

ISBN-13: 978-0-7377-4047-9
ISBN-10: 0-7377-4047-7

Printed in the United States of America
2 3 4 5 6 7 12 11 10 09 08

Contents

Chapter 1

Mysterious Designs

When crop circles started appearing regularly in the 1980s they usually looked like simple circles cut into crop fields, with the crops inside the circle pushed to the ground in a swirling pattern. They attracted a lot of attention because most people had never seen anything exactly like them before. Ninety percent of the circles appeared in southern England, although no one knew for sure why this happened. At the time, scientists and others developed various theories as to who or what created them, and how they were formed, but no one could find the answer.

Unlike other unexplained **phenomena**, such as ghosts, crop circles are visible for everyone to see. Their existence is not questionable. What they are and how they are created is a mystery.

The Natural History of Staffordshire

One of the first recorded incidents of a person watching a crop circle form is found in British author Richard Plott's 1686 book *The Natural History of Staffordshire.* Plott's book reports that in 1590 Nicolaea Lang-Berhand saw a group of people dancing in a field. Suddenly they all vanished, except for one person, "whom . . . she saw [blown] up into the Air . . . and [she] was also driven so forcibly with the wind, that it made her almost lose her breath."

She said that the wind was blowing so hard that it blew local herdsman John Michael out of the oak tree where he was sitting, and he was "presently [caught] up again with a whirlwind," and then dropped in a nearby meadow. After this happened, Plott wrote, "There was found in the place where they danced a round circle."[1]

The History of Crop Circles

There were few reports of crop circles until August 15, 1980, when three crop circles were discovered in a field of oats in Wiltshire, England. Curious sightseers drove out to the countryside to examine them, but no one really knew what to make of the circles that were 60 feet (20m) in diameter in the middle of the field. They were completely surrounded by undamaged oats, and there were no footprints or paths that would indicate people had made the circles.

Woodcut

A 17th-century woodcut of a crop circle called *The Devil Mower* appeared in a Hertfordshire, England, newspaper on August 22, 1678. The article said the formation was so neatly pressed that "no mortal man was able to do the like." It was therefore thought to have been done by the "devil or some infernal spirit."

The Mowing-Devil:

Or, Strange *NEWS* out of

Hartford-ſhire.

Being a True Relation of a Farmer, who Bargaining with a Poor *Mower*, about the Cutting down Three Half Acres of *Oats*; upon the *Mower's* asking too much, the *Farmer* ſwore, *That the Devil ſhould Mow it, rather than He.* And ſo it fell out, that that very Night, the Crop of *Oat* ſhew'd as if it had been all of a Flame; but next Morning appear'd ſo neatly Mow'd by the Devil, or ſome Infernal Spirit, that no Mortal Man was able to do the like.

Alſo, How the ſaid *Oats* ly now in the Field, and the Owner has not Power to fetch them away.

Licenſed, *Auguſt* 22th. 1678.

An illustration of a crop of oats being mowed by the devil appeared in a Hertfordshire, England, newspaper on August 22, 1678.

In many crop circles the crops are pressed down in such a precise pattern, with little or no damage to the stalks, that it seems hard to believe it could have been done by human hands.

John Scull, the farmer who owned the field, was astonished by their appearance, saying, "I have never seen marks like it before. It certainly can't be wind or rain damage, because I have seen plenty of that and it is just not that regular."[2]

He was referring to the fact that the crop stalks had been swirled down in the same direction, into a neat spiraling pattern. Also, the flattened stalks inside the circles were not damaged as they would be if someone had run farm machinery over them. They looked as if they had been gently pushed down to within an inch or two from the ground. It was a mystery who or what could have done something like that, and why they would do it.

After the August 15, 1980, crop circles appeared, they started appearing regularly in England during the summer months. They remained mostly simple circles cut into fields of crops that were usually discovered in the early morning, with the farmers claiming they were sure the circles were not in the fields the night before. Hundreds of people visited the fields to see the crop circles that had formed.

Some people started to conduct research on crop circles; they became known as crop circle researchers, sometimes more formally called cereologists. They recorded the air temperature inside the circles, measured their length, and studied what kind of weather had occurred that day. They also

Carved into Sand

Crop circles have appeared in surfaces other than fields. In July 1998 a gigantic figure of an aborigine appeared carved into the sand in a remote region of Australia. With a length of 2.4 miles (4km) it was so big that it could be seen from outer space. Every line of the figure was 39 yards (35m) wide. To construct the figure's outline with a plow, a tractor would have had to travel hundreds of miles.

noted where the circles formed and what the area's geography was like.

There were many people, however, who claimed that crop circles were **hoaxes**, created by people as a kind of prank. They said people could make the circles in many different ways. One suggestion was that a tall strong man could stand in the middle of the circle and swing a heavy weight around on a long piece of rope so that the crops were pushed down in the shape of a circle. Some doubted whether a person could create such large patterns so perfectly without being seen or heard while working in the field. Others argued the people making the crop circles would not be noticed if they worked in the middle of the night.

Complex Crop Circles

The ideas crop circle researchers and others had formed about the circles were challenged on July 12, 1990. That morning a loud rumbling sound was heard in Alton Barnes, in southern England. Dogs started barking and could not be calmed. When farmer Tim Carson went out to his fields in the early morning he saw a surprising sight: a huge, 555-foot-long (185m) crop circle formation made up of circles with rings around them. Sticking out of some of the rings were shapes that resembled long, old-fashioned skeleton keys.

Local resident Mary Killen was one of the hundreds of people who visited the formation that day.

Residents of Alton Barnes, England, awoke to discover this crop circle in a local farmer's field on July 12, 1990.

She said that the circles "were perfect, as if they'd been made in one fell swoop. I mean, there was no possibility of a human being doing that; it was too **geometrically** exact. Human error would have come into it if it had been made by a human."[3]

Local newspapers printed pictures and stories about the odd formation. These stories were also published later in larger papers all around the world. This caused more sightseers to rush to the field to examine the various shapes, and to see what it felt like to stand inside a crop circle. Some people reported suddenly feeling very tired, and they complained of pounding headaches. Others claimed they felt an intense sense of calm settle over them.

Meanwhile, researchers struggled to discover what could possibly have created a formation that was so massive and made up of different shapes. They wanted to know whether people could create such an elaborate design or if there was something mysterious at work. It was also unknown if the noise that had occurred that morning was connected to the formation. Researchers began testing different theories. They tested methods and tools that might create a complex crop circle in just a few hours; they studied the ground and the air around the crop circle to see if it had different and special properties.

Rare Daytime Eyewitness Encounter

Researchers had been studying the circle in Alton Barnes for just a few months when another unique event was reported in a different part of England. George and Vivienne Tomlinson were walking in a cornfield near Hambledon, England, when the plants started rustling around them.

"There was a mist hovering above, and we heard a high-pitched sound," said Vivienne Tomlinson.

Farmers Feared Ridicule

Crop circles were once thought to be caused by strange diseases, magic, and/or fairies. Because of this, farmers feared being ridiculed or even losing a buyer for their crop if they mentioned them, so they usually kept quiet about any crop circles they found in their fields.

> Then we felt wind pushing us from the side and above. It was forcing down on our heads so that we could hardly stay upright; yet my husband's hair was standing on end. It was incredible. Then the whirling air seemed to branch into two and zig-zagged off into the distance. We could still see it like a light mist or fog, shimmering as it moved.[4]

A crop circle formed in a nearby area.

Only about five or six dozen people have reported seeing crop circles form in the daytime. Some of them have also mentioned the high-pitched sound, whirling air, and the force that was present in the Tomlinsons' experience. Some researchers believe crop circles are formed by powerful swirling winds or whirlwinds. The Tomlinsons' report supports this idea.

Strange Designs

Most of the crop circles that were reported beginning with the 1990 summer season were complex formations that looked very different from the simple circles seen earlier. Some researchers called them **pictograms** because they looked similar to hieroglyphs, or pictures that represent words. Some of the shapes copied symbols from ancient civilizations. Some researchers wondered if there were messages in the patterns. Each year the formations grew increasingly complicated; some of the designs

This ant-shaped crop formation was discovered in Hampshire, England, in 1997.

contained intricate geometric shapes that many called works of art. Some formations resembled letters, symbols, and even huge bugs.

These complex formations attracted worldwide attention and inspired wonder and curiosity. The early circles were relatively small, but most of these newer ones were 200–300 feet (67–100m) in diameter. One was over 1,000 feet (333m) wide and had almost 200 circles. When these larger and more complex circles began to appear, researchers started doubting whether whirlwinds could create formations with so many different shapes.

Hoaxers

The following year, on September 9, 1991, two Englishmen, 67-year-old Doug Bower and 62-year-old Dave Chorley, announced that they had made all the crop circles that had been discovered, as a prank. They said they used a plank of wood and some string, and worked by the light of the moon. People who never believed that crop circles were magical or mysterious said the confession proved it was all a hoax.

Other groups admitted that they had also created some of the circles. One group, the Circlemakers, said that creating crop circles is an art. In 2002 they were hired by the History Channel to create a giant crop circle formation that was 140 feet (46m) in diameter.

Crop circle researchers responded by saying they had always suspected some circles were fakes because there were obvious differences from other circles they had examined. However, they also said the claims did not explain crop circles from the past, those discovered in remote areas around the world, or those that had appeared in the daytime.

Alien Evidence

Mysterious spacecraft, fast-moving balls of light in the sky, and domes of light the size of football fields have all been reported around crop circles. As hundreds of these reports piled up, people began trying to explain them. The detailed reports of witnesses, along with supposed pictures of flying craft near the crop circle sites have led some people to believe that extraterrestrials, or aliens, are responsible for creating crop circles.

Unidentified Flying Object (UFO) Sighted Near Crop Circle

On January 19, 1966, in the town of Tully in Queensland, Australia, George Pedley, a banana farmer, was driving his tractor across his property when he suddenly heard a strange hissing noise. He followed the sound to the neighboring property, which belonged to Albert Pennisi.

Pennisi relates what happened next:

> Suddenly George saw this blue-green machine rise up from our **lagoon**. It rose about 30–40 feet (9–12m) and then it turned on its side and just shot away. It was gone, vanished into thin air. George said anyone who saw it will tell you whatever made it was not of this world.

This circular mass of reeds, woven into a swirling clockwise design, was spotted floating on top of a lagoon on January 19, 1966, in the town of Tully in Queensland, Australia.

Entrance Fees

Some people believe that farmers pay artists to create crop circles on their property. They can then charge entrance fees to tour groups who want to see the circles.

> George went to the lagoon straight away and he saw the water still swirling, still churning around. I think it really shook him up, and he came to get me. . . . We went to the lagoon together and, by crikey, did I get a shock.[5]

Floating on top of the lagoon was a circular mass of reeds 29.5 feet (9m) across. They were tightly woven into a swirling clockwise design. Pennisi said it was sturdy enough to support the weight of ten men.

Similar circles appeared in the lagoon in 1972, 1975, 1980, 1982, and 1987. This area had long been known for UFO sightings, but not for the circles, which locals called "saucer nests." The local police, as well as the Royal Australian Air Force, conducted investigations, but they could not determine who or what was making the circles.

Hovering Saucers

Another UFO sighting near crop circles happened on September 1, 1974. At about 11 o'clock that

Many sightings of mysterious flying aircraft have been reported near areas where crop circles have appeared.

morning 36-year-old Edwin Fuhr was harvesting his crop near Langenburg, Saskatchewan, Canada, when he noticed what appeared to be a metallic dome about 50 feet (17m) away from him. He left his harvester running and walked to within 15 feet (3m) of the object. It appeared to be an upside-down stainless-steel bowl, about 11 feet (4m) across and 5 feet (1.7m) high, and it was spinning rapidly. It was about 12 to 18 inches (30 to 46cm) above the ground.

Looking around, Fuhr realized there were four similar objects, all rotating quickly. Suddenly, all five objects rose into the air to a height of above 200 feet (67m) and stopped. Then they shot up and disappeared into a low-flying cloud. Fuhr said a "pressure flattened the crop that was standing, and there was just a downward wind, no twirling wind. I had to hold onto my hat." He also reported a period of momentary paralysis while in the presence of the phenomenon. Fuhr said, "My head wanted to go back fast, but my feet didn't want to move. . . . I sat there like I was froze. I couldn't move."

After the objects left, Fuhr found five circles spiraled flat in a clockwise direction. "I checked for burns," he said, "but I couldn't find any."[6]

Many similar sightings have been reported by people who seemed to have nothing to gain by their statements. In fact, crop circle researchers say many people have anonymously reported similar incidents, but they do not want to make public statements for fear others will not believe them or will make fun of them.

Domes of Light

Besides spacecraft, huge domes of light have been spotted where crop circles have later appeared. While crop circles are usually found the same day that strange lights are reported, sometimes there

Silbury Hill in Wiltshire, England, is the tallest prehistoric man-made mound in Europe. It is also an area known for crop circles. This crop formation was photographed in 2000.

are delays. On July 13, 1988, for example, around 11:30 P.M. Mary Freeman was driving near Silbury Hill in southern England when she noticed that a large cloud in the sky ahead had an odd, golden-white glow on its underside.

Then, to her surprise an oval object appeared right at the same part of the cloud. Suddenly, a beam of light as wide as a football field shot out from the object, aimed at the ground below. When it happened, all the loose objects in Freeman's car **levitated** around her, almost as if her car had been caught up in an energy field of some sort. Amazed at what she was seeing, she sped toward the light. The oval object stayed in place for about three minutes

Natural Phenomenon

Some scientists believe the strange lights that people sometimes report could be ball lightning. These compact balls of energy can take numerous forms, ranging from one inch (2.5cm) to five feet (1.5m) in diameter. However, they most commonly appear as small, luminous spheres up to fifteen inches (38cm) in diameter. They can move freely and exist for up to ten minutes.

before it disappeared. Within thirty-six hours a crop circle formation with five Celtic crosses (a cross similar to the Latin cross with a ring at the intersection of the crossbar) appeared at the base of Silbury Hill. Freeman called the experience "ethereal."[7]

Others have also reported seeing these huge domes of light. One summer night in 1997 Jack Spooner was driving in the countryside in Dorset, England, when he saw something amazing. "A large dome of light, about 200 feet (67m) in diameter, was touching the corn field. There were thousands of points of light, like diamonds, all aligned and geometric. It was glistening, shimmering like a hologram."[8] He also heard a high-pitched sound. However, when he got closer, and his headlights illuminated the area, the dome disappeared and the noise stopped.

The next morning two half rings of flattened crop appeared on the spot where Spooner had seen the dome of light. He thought that perhaps if the light from his car had not lit up the area that a more elaborate pattern might have developed.

Strange, Unnatural Lights

There have been widespread reports from reliable witnesses of strange lights in the sky the night before crop circles appear. Many of these people say these lights were far too low to the ground, and flew at such high speeds, that they could not possibly have been airplanes or other conventional flying objects.

In his book *Secrets in the Fields*, crop circle researcher Freddy Silva cites two such examples of mysterious lights in England. "In 1990, the night before forty circles appeared in East Anglia, there were reports of orange lights as large as the full moon. Also, at Devon a circle with seven satellites appeared soon after a bullet-shaped object with

Many witnesses have reported seeing strange lights in the sky the night before crop circles appear.

Earth's Electrical Energy

Another possible explanation for the strange lights is the tectonic strain theory. According to this theory, massive stresses within the Earth's crust generate electrical energy that is discharged into the atmosphere. This creates balls of plasma that give off light. In tests, rocks subjected to high pressure generate electricity that can be discharged as light. More testing is needed to advance this theory.

rows of colored lights was reported flying silently across the area."[9]

Another witness reported seeing small, brilliant white lights flying close to where a circle was later discovered. He said they looked like balls of light that seemed to fade in and out. They did not seem like any kind of natural phenomena. Similar statements have been recorded where witnesses said it appeared that the lights could become visible or invisible at will. Believers say this suggests that they are guided by some kind of intelligence. Besides, they ask, if these lights are not UFOs, what else could they be?

Special Energy

Powerful energy force fields and some type of presence that seems to respond to human thoughts and voices have been reported within crop circles. Some people have said it is as if the crop circles themselves come alive. This can be disturbing, because people have no idea what kind of danger they may be in, or what forces they are dealing with, as seen in the following situations.

Black Flash

In late June 1987 crop circle researcher Colin Andrews was sitting inside a crop circle about 30 feet (10m) in diameter that was located near Andover, England. It had formed a few weeks earlier, on

Crop circle researcher Colin Andrews, pictured in the 1980s, is one of the leading authorities on the subject of crop formations.

June 13th. Two young boys told him they had seen a strange, glowing orange object hovering in the area the night before the circle had formed. Also, a few local elderly villagers said they had heard strange "warbling, humming-like noises" that same night. Mr. Flambert, the farmer who owned the field, was astounded at the sight of the circle, saying, "I've never seen anything like this before."[10]

Andrews had seen dozens of crop circles by then, and they continued to fascinate him. That day he was dictating some observations into a tape recorder when he suddenly experienced what he called a "black flash" all around him.

"I flinched and for a fraction of a second the sky was blotted out. At once I looked up into the sky. There was nothing in front of the sun,"[11] Andrews said.

That afternoon Andrews returned to the area with his dog. Someone had once suggested to him that animals can sense things that humans cannot. He wanted to see if his dog could detect any residual energy in the circle. If it did, that might explain what had happened to him that morning. Unfortunately,

Crop Circle Experiences

Some people believe that crop circles interact at an unconscious or telepathic (the ability to communicate or read someone's mind without using words or physical signals) level, and that a person's experience in a crop circle is determined largely by his or her state of mind.

it worked in a way that Andrews had not anticipated. Within minutes of entering the circle, his dog vomited and became quite ill. Andrews immediately took the dog home, where it quickly returned to normal.

Curious as to what forces or energies were at work within the circle, Andrews returned to the circle again that evening. For years he had struggled to find answers that would explain the crop circle phenomenon. He desperately wanted to unlock their secrets; he wanted to know who or what made them, and how they were formed. He felt overwhelmingly frustrated. At that moment he looked up at the sky and pleaded that he somehow be allowed to discover the answers.

According to Andrews, just then an

> electrical crackling noise started to come from a spot about nine feet away. It grew louder, up to a pitch where I expected a bang to follow. Frightened, I looked toward the village to check my quickest route out of the field. I fought to [control] my panic and remained still. Then, as suddenly as it had started, it stopped. It had lasted about six seconds, although it seemed longer.[12]

Shaken, he stayed where he was until he calmed down. He had heard the electrical noise before, but this time it seemed to be dangerously directed at him. He wondered exactly how powerful this force could be.

Operation White Crow

Andrews was not alone. There were others who thought powerful forces were at work within the crop circles. Some were determined to find out what they were. Because of this, Andrews and other leading crop circle researchers organized what they called the first major crop watch in June 1989 at Cheesefoot Head, England. The project was called Operation White Crow. The researchers were all eager to see if anything would develop during the session. Cheesefoot Head had been the site of dozens of crop circle formations over the years, so it seemed like a likely place to hold the event. Participants were equipped with night-vision cameras, video recorders, and meteorological equipment, ready to record anything that happened, day or night.

Crop circle researchers gather at Cheesefoot Head, Hampshire, England, to investigate a crop formation.

Objective Observers?

Some criticized participants of Operation White Crow, saying the participants were not very objective going into the study. They say there is no evidence that a person or persons participating in the crop watch had not created the crop circle in the neighboring field, simply to make it look as if the crop watch had not failed in its efforts.

Unfortunately, except for the sighting one morning of an orange light in the sky, nothing unusual occurred in the area they were watching. The disappointed researchers took a different approach. They decided to try to directly contact whatever spirit or intelligence that might be controlling the circles. So, on the final day of the crop watch, some of the members sat in the middle of a nearby crop circle that had formed a few weeks earlier, with psychic Rita Goold, hoping that some of the circle's energy would still be there. Goold went into a trance, and at her direction the others closed their eyes and directed their thoughts and questions to the circle.

Suddenly, they said, there was an incredibly loud noise that sounded like the crackling of high electrical voltage wires. At first it seemed to be on one side of them, but then it moved around until it had encircled them. A few of the people became anxious, wondering what would happen next. Then, according to their reports, crop circle researcher Pat Delgado was dragged into the center of the circle by an invisible force. He tried to fight against it but could not. It bent him backwards at an unnatural angle, and then started dragging him around the circle. Everyone there witnessed the event.

"No!" he gasped. "No!"

Trying to help, Goold shouted, "If you can understand us, stop."[13] Soon afterwards the noise and force field stopped, and Delgado was hurled to the ground.

Shortly afterwards they heard the noise again. It seemed to be moving down the field. The group quickly debated if they dared followed it. Finally, two men hurried forward, trying to catch up with the noise. They walked all the way downhill until they reached a barbed wire fence. Here they were forced to stop, because it blocked their path. They learned later that a crop circle had formed in the next field.

Electrical Interference

Later that same summer, in August 1989, Delgado and Colin Andrews were with a British Broadcasting Company (BBC) crew, getting ready to tape a talk about their crop circle research and their new book, *Circular Evidence*, which was about to be released. Everyone was standing in a massive 120 foot (40m) circle near Beckhamptom, England.

They were delayed because a problem had suddenly developed with the BBC's video camera. Red lights on its instrument panel indicated there was some kind of electrical malfunction. The problem went away when they moved the camera out of the circle, but returned when they moved it back in again. They eventually had to switch to another camera so they could start shooting.

Then, a loud buzzing sound started. Delgado, who was in the middle of the circle, said, "I can feel it. It's right here."[14] He motioned with his hands to

In 1989 a British television crew experienced unexplained electrical interference while filming from within a crop circle. Other strange occurrences have been reported by those who have ventured into a crop circle.

Ruined Tires

Farmers have reported that their heavy-duty tractor tires, which were designed to outlast the life of the farm machinery, have deflated inside of crop circles. In Surrey, England, three tires, belonging to two different machines, experienced a collapse of their metal structures.

indicate the noise was coming from the ground beneath his feet. He stepped out of the circle, and the noise stopped. When he stepped back in, the noise started again.

Afterwards, the camera had to be completely rebuilt, and the cause of the noise interference was never found. When the show aired on British television, it earned high ratings and was said to turn many nonbelievers into crop circle believers.

Unexplainable incidents like this happened regularly within the crop circles. Researchers have proposed many different ideas as to what causes them, but no one idea seems to totally explain the phenomenon. While some believe the answer will eventually be found through scientific research, others believe the truth might lie in a different direction.

Ancient Sites and Crop Circles

Most crop circles appear near ancient sites. This is particularly true in England. Some crop circle researchers believe the circles are attracted to the geographical "hot spots" of Earth energy that these monuments and landmarks are said to occupy. It may be that this mysterious energy causes strange things to happen in and around crop circles.

Stonehenge Crop Circle Formation

Stonehenge is a famous prehistoric site in Wiltshire, England. Massive rectangular stones are arranged in a circular pattern at the site. Some think the ancient site was used as an astronomical observatory and was also a place where rituals were held. However, no one knows this for sure. It is a very busy place; every day busloads of people come from all over the world to see it.

On July 7, 1996, in late afternoon, a huge crop circle formation that looked like a complicated geometric pattern appeared directly across from Stonehenge. The huge formation was named the Julia Set. It was 920 feet (307m) long and 500 feet (167m) wide, and had 151 separate circles that varied from 1 foot (.3m) to 50 feet (17m) in diameter.

The crop circle that appeared across from Stonehenge on July 7, 1996, pictured, has been called the greatest crop circle formation of all time. Its complicated pattern contains 151 separate circles.

It has been called one of the greatest crop circle formations of all time. A comparison of reports filed by patrolling Stonehenge security guards, as well as pilots who flew over the formation in late afternoon, indicated the complex crop circle formation was created within only a thirty-minute period.

Although the crop circle formation appeared in broad daylight only 656 feet (200m) from Stonehenge, a major tourist attraction that has hundreds of tourists walking around it every day, nobody reported seeing anyone or anything create the circle. Likewise, no one who drove on the busy superhighway that runs between Stonehenge and the Julia Set formation reported seeing anyone or anything creating the formation.

Mr. Sandell, the farmer who owned the field, claimed that he had personally inspected the field

Dragon Energy

An early reference to a kind of Earth energy appeared in the first century A.D. Greek biographer Plutarch referred to streams of Earth energy called dragon energy that were influenced by the Sun and celestial bodies that activated oracles and other important places.

that morning and had found nothing unusual. At first, after the formation appeared, he wanted to deny crop circle researchers and curious sightseers access to the formation. He was angry, because from ground level all he could see was that his crop had been cut up, so he thought vandals had done it. However, when someone showed him an aerial photo of the formation, he changed his mind, saying, "People can't make that." He placed a big sign at the field's entrance that said, "See Europe's best crop circle,"[15] and charged a small entrance fee.

Stories and pictures of the formation were published in newspapers and magazines all over the world. Over the next three weeks approximately ten thousand people visited the site, eager to see the crop circle that had mysteriously appeared there.

Crop circle researcher Freddy Silva visited the formation shortly after it appeared. He said, "It took a team of eleven people five hours just to survey the formation. Over the course of the hot afternoon, our presence attracted the curiosity of dozens of motorists as well as a small crowd at Stonehenge. How humans making this circle could have avoided detection is beyond me."[16]

He thought it was interesting that after visiting the formation a molecular biologist said he experienced sensations similar to intense ultraviolet radiation or gamma radiation exposure. The man said he felt nauseous, but after sleeping he felt an "intense physical well-being and mental clarity."[17]

Earth Energy

Feelings like this have been mentioned by others who enter crop circles. Some people believe that the circles have somehow tapped into some as yet unknown but powerful Earth energies. Centuries-old stories and myths say that ancient sites like Stonehenge and Silbury Hill are also places where these energies have been unlocked.

Some researchers believe that people built Stonehenge and other ancient sites where they did because they had discovered those were places of power, where Earth's energy was extremely strong. It is possible that the Stonehenge builders wanted to harness the power so people could go there to experience it.

Some researchers believe that people built Stonehenge, pictured, and other ancient sites where they did because they had discovered those were places where Earth's energy was extremely strong.

Earth Energies

A number of ancient societies have sought out Earth energies. According to writer Jim Schnabel, "The Druids are said to have built temples around it. The Buddhists are supposed to have represented it by their serpent-figure, Kundalini, and the Chinese are said to have recognized it in their mysterious science of feng-shui, in which yin and yang currents of earth-energy are mapped out, built around, harnessed and harmonized."

It is also an old tradition for people who hoped to be healed of a physical illness to walk through and around ancient sites. Crop circle researcher Lucy Pringle was amazed when she experienced this same healing in a crop circle when she walked into one with a serious shoulder injury, and felt the pain totally disappear while she was there.

This Earth energy may even extend up into the air over the circles. Crop circle researcher Freddy Silva flew in a small plane over a set of new crop formations in 2000 near Silbury Hill. He took aerial photos of the formations below. When the negatives were developed, all the images were normal, except for a row of nine frames in the middle. "Either side of these, the images show my approach and departure from Silbury Hill. The pictures I took when I was above the formations were blank."[18]

Ley Lines

There is one prominent theory that might explain this unknown Earth energy. In his 1925 book *The Old Straight Tack,* Alfred Watkins proposed that ancient monuments and other landmarks were deliberately built, or aligned, in more or less straight lines that he called **ley lines**, which crossed the English countryside. He believed they may have been set up to help ancient merchants and other travelers find their way around prehistoric Britain.

In the 1960s scholar John Mitchell researched Watkins's ideas and suggested that the lines were much more than road maps for traders. He believed they were lines of Earth energy, something the Chinese called **lung mei**, or dragon paths. He believed that ancient people knew about these strange Earth forces. Mitchell also observed that multiple ley lines intersected at Stonehenge. He suggested that the power is dramatically increased at locations where this happens. Interestingly, researchers have found that multiple ley lines often cross within crop formations as well.

More Research Needed

Many questions remain unanswered about crop circles. It is possible that people currently do not have

In 1923 Alfred Watkins claimed that this pathway in Llanthony, Wales, was evidence of an ancient pathway built along a ley line, or line of Earth energy.

the technology to answer them. Until more research is done, the true nature of crop circles will remain a mystery. In the meantime, thousands of people are likely to visit the crop circles that appear each summer, curious as to what they will find.

Notes

Chapter 1: Mysterious Designs

1. Quoted in Jerome Clark, *Unexplained! Strange Sightings, Incredible Occurrences and Puzzling Phenomena.* Canton, MI: Visible Ink, 1999, p. 151.
2. Quoted in Jim Schnabel, *Round in Circles.* New York: Prometheus, 1994, p. 7.
3. Quoted in Schnabel, *Round in Circles,* p. 158.
4. Quoted in Clark, *Unexplained! Strange Sightings, Incredible Occurrences and Puzzling Phenomena,* p. 150.

Chapter 2: Alien Evidence

5. Quoted in Frances Whiting, "Circles' Birthplace," Circlemakers. www.circlemakers.org/ tully.html.
6. Quoted in Clark, *Unexplained! Strange Sightings, Incredible Occurrences and Puzzling Phenomena,* p. 153.
7. Quoted in Schnabel, *Round in Circles,* p. 61.
8. Quoted in Freddy Silva, *Secrets in the Fields.* Charlottesville, VA: Hampton Roads, 2002, p. 137.
9. Quoted in Silva, *Secrets in the Fields,* p. 22.

Chapter 3: Special Energy

10. Quoted in Silva, *Secrets in the Fields,* p. 11.
11. Quoted in Schnabel, *Round in Circles,* p. 44.
12. Quoted in Silva, *Secrets in the Fields,* p. 11.

13. Quoted in Schnabel, *Round in Circles*, p. 107.
14. Quoted in Schnabel, *Round in Circles*, pp. 120–21.

Chapter 4: Ancient Sites and Crop Circles

15. Quoted in Silva, *Secrets in the Fields*, p. 74.
16. Quoted in Silva, *Secrets in the Fields*, p. 75.
17. Quoted in Silva, *Secrets in the Fields*, p. 76.
18. Quoted in Silva, *Secrets in the Fields*, p. 243.

aborigine: A member of the first people known to have lived in Australia.

geometrically: Shapes formed of straight lines or curves, such as triangles, rectangles, and circles.

hoaxes: Things that are meant to trick or fool others.

lagoon: A shallow lake or pond.

levitated: Rose and floated in the air.

ley lines: Lines that are believed to be a network of paths by which prehistoric people journeyed about Britain. They have also been called energy paths on the Earth's surface.

lung mei: Dragon paths, or paths of Earth energy, also known as ley lines.

phenomena: Remarkable or unexplained happenings.

pictograms: Primitive drawings.

For Further Exploration

Books

Jan Burns, *Crop Circles.* Detroit, MI: Lucent, 2006. This book offers different theories about how crop circles are formed.

Michael Martin, *Crop Circles.* Mankato, MN: Capstone, 2006. An easy-to-understand book with basic information about crop circles.

Chris Oxlade, *The Mystery of Crop Circles.* Chicago: Heinemann Library, 2006. This book covers basic information about crop circles.

Freddy Silva, *Secrets in the Fields.* Charlottesville, VA: Hampton Roads, 2002. Freddy Silva has researched crop circles for years. This book offers an in-depth look at crop circles and formations.

Colin Wilson and Damon Wilson, *The Mammoth Encyclopedia of the Unsolved.* New York: Carroll & Graf, 2000. This presents a good general overview of crop circles.

Web Sites

Crop Circle Quest (www.cropcirclequest.com). This site has links to articles about crop circles, the Canadian crop circle research network, England's crop circle network, and top ongoing scientific investigations.

Crop Circles Research (www.cropcircleinfo.com). This site offers an interesting and informative look at Colin Andrews's crop circle research. He was one of the first crop circle researchers.

Index

Picture Credits

Cover photo: © Paul Chinn/San Francisco Chronicle/Corbis
AP Images, 7
© The British Library/HIP/The Image Works, 6
EH/RCHME staff photographer (creator), © English Heritage. NMR/Heritage Images/The Image Works, 35
Fortean Picture Library, 13, 16
© Fortean/Topham/The Image Works, 20
© Mary Evans Picture Library/The Image Works, 18, 23, 41
© Mary Evans Picture Library/Stacy Collection, 26, 29, 32
Susan D. Rock, 38
© Topham/The Image Works, 10

About the Author

Jan Burns writes books, articles, and short stories for children and adults. She has a bachelor's degree in sociology from the University of California-Berkeley. She lives near Houston, Texas, with her husband, Don, and sons, David and Matt.